Way of Life
Participant Guide

WAY OF LIFE:
A STUDY BASED ON
THE GREAT SPIRITUAL MIGRATION

Way of Life Participant Guide

978-1-5018-4769-1
978-1-5018-4770-7 ebook

Way of Life: DVD

978-1-5018-4773-8

Way of Life: Leader Guide

978-1-5018-4771-4
978-1-5018-4772-1 ebook

The Great Spiritual Migration:
How the World's Largest Religion
Is Seeking a Better Way to Be Christian

978-1-60142-791-5 Hardcover
978-1-6014-2792-2 Paperback
978-1-60142-793-9 ebook

WAY OF LIFE

A STUDY BASED ON
THE GREAT SPIRITUAL MIGRATION

BRIAN D. McLAREN

Participant Guide
by Maria Mayo

Abingdon Press / Nashville

WAY OF LIFE
A Study Based on *The Great Spiritual Migration*

Copyright © 2017 Abingdon Press

All rights reserved.

978-1-5018-4769-1

Scripture quotations unless noted otherwise are taken from the Common English Bible, copyright 2011. Used by permission. All rights reserved.

Scripture quotations marked (ESV) are from the ESV Bible (The Holy Bible, English Standard Version™), copyright © 2001 by Crossway, a publishing ministry of Good News Publishers. Used by permission. All rights reserved.

Scripture quotations marked (KJV) are from The Authorized (King James) Version. Rights in the Authorized Version in the United Kingdom are vested in the Crown. Reproduced by permission of the Crown's patentee, Cambridge University Press.

Scripture quotations marked (NIV) are taken from the Holy Bible, New International Version™, NIV™. Copyright © 1973, 1978, 1984, 2011 by Biblica, Inc.™ Used by permission of Zondervan. All rights reserved worldwide. www.zondervan.com. The "NIV" and "New International Version" are trademarks registered in the United States Patent and Trademark Office by Biblica, Inc.™

Scripture quotations marked (NRSV) are taken from the New Revised Standard Version Bible, copyright © 1989 National Council of the Churches of Christ in the United States of America. Used by permission. All rights reserved worldwide. http://nrsvbibles.org/

Based on *The Great Spiritual Migration: How the World's Largest Religion Is Seeking a Better Way to Be Christian.* Copyright © 2016 by Brian D. McLaren. All rights reserved. Published in the United States by Convergent Books, an imprint of the Crown Publishing Group, a division of Penguin Random House LLC, New York. crownpublishing.com

17 18 19 20 21 22 23 24 25 26 — 10 9 8 7 6 5 4 3 2 1
MANUFACTURED IN THE UNITED STATES OF AMERICA

Contents

Introduction

Introduction

Migration is the seasonal movement, often between north and south, of many species of birds. Driven primarily by the availability of food, migration patterns have been recorded for thousands of years, even in Scripture. Job 39:26 reads, "Is it by your wisdom that the hawk soars, and spreads its wings toward the south?" (NRSV). Like hawks and geese and other birds, we human beings feel an innate urge that pushes us to roam. Anthropologists tell us that our species has been migrating for around two hundred thousand years. From our evolutionary birthplace in East Africa, our most ancient ancestors spread west and south across Africa, then north across the Middle East, some then heading west across Europe and others heading east across Asia, eventually arriving in North America and quickly spreading through Central and South America. Even now above us, human beings have migrated to space, and many of us dream of voyages to distant planets and even to other stars. To be human is to move. To be human is to change.

Today, Christianity is in need of movement and change. In *The Great Spiritual Migration*, Brian McLaren lays out his strategy for how millions of Christian believers can move the faith to a better place and become better Christians. He explains three powerful shifts that define the change.

First, McLaren argues that Christianity has reduced its core identity to a collection of correct beliefs. Beliefs are interesting and important, he says, but a list of unchanging beliefs should not define what it means to be a follower of Christ. Instead, he advocates for a way of life centered on love, following the example of Jesus' life and teaching, which he calls "the way of life of love." Throughout the New Testament, he says, love is the main thing, the one thing that matters above all others. The spiritual migration, then, is a challenge to Christians to live into the good news of Jesus Christ in their daily lives, and to understand Christianity as a way of life, a way of love.

In the second section, "The Theological Migration," McLaren explores the theological shift that must take place if we are to live into this new way of life. Some passages of Scripture reveal God to be vengeful and violent, favoring some people and disfavoring or rejecting others. As a result of this portrayal, some Christians have felt justified in perpetrating much violence in the world. Such violence—and such a violent concept of God—must become unacceptable for us as we move forward. We must move toward the loving God, whose character emerges as the Scriptural story unfolds in both the Old and New Testaments, revealed in Jesus as One who is for all of us and not against any of us. He challenges us to leave behind methods of interpreting Scripture that hinder that vision of a loving God from shining through. The life and work of Jesus show us a generous and loving God, who is the Spirit of justice, joy, and peace, and this is the God who empowers us to a new way of life based on love.

The third section, "The Missional Migration," is a call to action. The move toward a new way of life starts with individuals and groups adopting the new way of thinking about beliefs, Scripture, and God. McLaren draws on social movement theory to show

how Christians (and those of all faiths) can join together to turn organized religion (religion organized for self-perpetuation) into organizing religion (religion organizing for the common good). He portrays the ministry of Jesus as a social and spiritual movement in which we are invited to participate.

Through these three migrations, McLaren offers concrete suggestions for individuals, congregations, and other groups to help them rethink their conception of Christian faith, of God, and of the practice of religion, and to migrate to a new way of life based on love.

In this Participant Guide, you'll find summaries of the book's four sections, considerations of Scripture, questions for reflection, and excerpts with questions for personal contemplation. Also included are four previously unpublished devotions written by Brian McLaren that reflect on the themes in each section. The study is organized into four sessions covering the book's introduction and three sections. This book functions as a tour guide for *The Great Spiritual Migration*, providing explanations and prompting deeper thought about McLaren's work.

Let this study serve as a convening table around which we can begin the conversation about the loving way of life embodied by Jesus—the nonviolent, liberating spirit of God—and how we can all become reflections of Christ in the world, working together for the common good.

Session 1

A Better Way
to Be Christian

Session 1

A Better Way to Be Christian

SUMMARY

Introduction: Coke and the Can

In the introduction to *The Great Spiritual Migration*, Brian McLaren makes a bold claim: Christianity is in need of change. It needs a migration, he says, from a system of beliefs to a way of life based on love. I'm sure some of you are asking, Isn't Christianity already a way of life based on love? According to McLaren, the way of life set forth by Jesus in the Gospels has been redefined as a system of beliefs, a system that has sometimes supported harmful actions and ideologies. He goes on to identify three migrations needed to transform Christianity: spiritual, theological, and missional. The first migration moves Christianity from a system of beliefs to a way of life of love. Rather than an expression of faith in action, McLaren says, Christianity has become a list of beliefs or tenets that define what it means to be Christian. He argues that Christianity needs to stop holding on so tightly to its beliefs and start focusing on the faith, the truth, and the way of life that Jesus embodied so many centuries ago.

This return to a way of life of love set out by Jesus comes with a second migration, a theological shift. Just as Christianity has been defined as a system of beliefs, God has grown large as a Supreme Being who blesses and punishes in equal measure. According to McLaren, Christians must migrate to a new vision of God, one that reigns over the way of life of love and demonstrates the kind of loving, healing, and reconciling spirit that Jesus proclaimed. A God who is punishing and dominating does not match up with the God of Jesus, who eats with sinners, welcomes outsiders, takes the role of a servant, and forgives without bound. This is the God we need, and this is the God of Jesus: the God of the way of life of love.

Christianity defined as a way of life with a God who is loving and reconciling needs just one more migration. This missional migration involves a new understanding of communities and institutions that are flexible and transformative. What Christianity needs, says McLaren, is a mature openness to change and adaptation. We need a Christianity that is willing to transform itself, over and over. We should challenge our institutions to learn and grow, ever moving toward a new vision of God and a way of life of love.

With these three migrations as *spiritual*—moving away from a system of beliefs and toward Christianity as a way of life, *theological*—thinking anew about Scripture and rediscovering a vision of a loving God, and *missional*, or *practical*—going from an organized religion to a religion organizing itself for the common good, McLaren sounds the call for a new way of thinking about Christian identity.

The introduction begins with this parable about a can of Coke: You call customer service and report that your Coke tastes terrible. The customer service agent asks about the appearance of the can, and you say that it looks shiny and red and normal. The customer service agent says that's the most important thing and then asks about the cardboard box that held the cans. You reply that it was also perfectly normal, with all the logos in the right place. The customer service agent says that everything sounds fine and thanks you for calling! In this parable, we see someone completely miss the point—it's what's inside the can that matters, not the can or the packaging. What if we applied the same principle to Christianity? What are the qualities of Christianity that really matter, aside from all the institutions and structures and systems of belief?

SCRIPTURE REFLECTION

Dear friends, I wanted very much to write to you concerning the salvation we share. Instead, I must write to urge you to fight for the faith delivered once and for all to God's holy people.

Jude 1:3

Compete in the good fight of faith. Grab hold of eternal life—you were called to it, and you made a good confession of it in the presence of many witnesses.

1 Timothy 6:12

"How terrible it will be for you legal experts and Pharisees! Hypocrites! You clean the outside of the cup and plate, but inside they are full of violence and pleasure seeking. Blind Pharisee! First clean the

*inside of the cup so that the outside of the cup will
be clean too.*

*"How terrible it will be for you legal experts and
Pharisees! Hypocrites! You are like whitewashed
tombs. They look beautiful on the outside. But inside
they are full of dead bones and all kinds of filth.
In the same way you look righteous to people. But
inside you are full of pretense and rebellion.*

Matthew 23:25-28

Have you ever competed in a fierce athletic contest? Maybe contended against some of the best runners in a 10K, or fought down to the last point in a championship basketball game? This is the kind of fighting that Jude is getting at when he counsels his readers to fight for the faith. In fact, the Greek word he uses is most often used when talking about intense effort in the context of athletics. Christianity is worth fighting for.

The metaphor of an athletic challenge used to describe the fight for faith is not unique to Jude. Paul uses the same language in 1 Timothy: "Compete in the good fight of faith. Grab hold of eternal life." "Compete," "fight," and "grab hold" are all physical images that demonstrate the kind of strength and determination it takes to fight for one's faith. Both Paul and Jude use the same Greek word for "compete" and "fight": *agonizomai*. Look closely: this is also the root of the English word "agony." It's a powerful and meaningful and gut-wrenching task to fight for one's faith.

In *The Great Spiritual Migration*, Brian McLaren lays out a modern-day concern much like Paul and Jude's—Christianity has suffered at the hands of Christians, has become a rigid system of beliefs, and no longer reflects the way of life of love taught by Jesus.

Note that Jude and Paul urge believers to fight for faith, not for systems of beliefs. Christianity is in danger of being lost, but this way of life of love is worth fighting for. It's a race worth winning, and we as Christians should put our most intense effort forward, agonizing as it may be. Think back to that all-important race or championship game. Fighting for the faith means fighting with that kind of strength and determination.

In the passage from the Gospel of Matthew, Jesus offers fighting words to his listeners. The verses here take the form of woe oracles, which were often used by the Old Testament prophets to castigate and accuse. The audience is not necessarily just the Pharisees, but anyone listening to Jesus' pronouncements, and further, anyone reading Matthew's Gospel. The warnings concern the mismatch of inner and outer characteristics, much like the short parable of the Coke and the can offered by McLaren. It is a mistake to focus only on the outer appearance of things. A sparkling clean cup and plate might still hold violence and pleasure seeking. Whitewashed tombs look clean and beautiful, but they are full of death and impurity. The same is true for Jesus' audience, he says. "You look righteous to people. But inside you are full of pretense and rebellion."

Jesus speaks out against hypocrisy and urges his listeners to match the contents with the container. Brian McLaren tells his story of the Coke can for the same reason. What are the qualities of Christianity that matter regardless of the building, the structures, or the systems of belief? On the outside, Christianity might look very good, but McLaren challenges us to look deep inside and see how things appear. Christianity, he maintains, has focused on polishing and perfecting its outer wrappings without addressing the troubling theology and beliefs that have grown up in its core.

QUESTIONS FOR REFLECTION

1. What do you think of the idea that Christianity needs to "migrate" to something new? Is that an uncomfortable idea? Why or why not?

2. McLaren writes, "We all love Jesus. To us, he is the best thing about Christianity. We all think he was right, and we all want to follow the way of life he modeled and taught." In your own religious tradition, how is following Jesus already taking place? What is lacking?

3. How might McLaren use the image of an athletic contest to describe his call for migration? Where does he seem to identify the need for a "fight"?

4. Imagine ways you can fight for your faith in today's world. Simply speaking about your convictions to other people could be a form of advocating for your faith. When was the last time you talked to someone about Jesus?

5. In what way(s) is McLaren fighting for Christianity?

6. Do you know anyone who has left the Christian faith or is close to doing so? What has driven them away?

7. In response to Jude 1:3, McLaren writes, "The message of and about Jesus is in fact a given—it is Christianity's pearl, our treasure, our gift, and it must never be lost. The meaning-rich stories of what Jesus said and did form the unique heart of Christian faith that must always pulse within us." What "meaning-rich stories of what Jesus said and did" are most important to your own faith? How would you summarize "the message of and about Jesus" in just one or two sentences?

8. Some people interpret Jude's mention of a "faith delivered once and for all" as proof that Christianity is

meant to stay the same throughout history. How do you understand that part of this verse?

9. What if one of your non-Christian friends asked you, What does it mean that Jesus taught a way of life of love? How would you explain? What examples would you use? What is the modern-day expression of the way of life of love?

10. McLaren shares this quotation: "A religion will be what its adherents make of it." Offer your reflections on that statement.

Personal Response

It is tempting to leave Christian faith altogether, I know. But there is a treasure hidden in its field, and I want to assure you that you have permission to shovel away the distractions and rediscover the precious gift that has for too long been buried. That's my good news: you don't have to give up on Christian faith. Nor do you have to accept it as it is. Christian faith can be saved, and you are invited to participate in its conversion.

-from *The Great Spiritual Migration*, Introduction

> "Again, the kingdom of heaven is like a merchant in search of fine pearls. When he found one very precious pearl, he went and sold all that he owned and bought it."
>
> Matthew 13:45-46

The above excerpt from *The Great Spiritual Migration* presents a hopeful vision for the future of Christianity. McLaren doesn't want to debunk or devalue Christianity; he wants to save it. He believes that a great conversion can happen and Christianity can become the way of life of love that it was meant to be. He invites all Christians to grab hold of their love for Jesus and come along for the ride.

Reflect on your response to the above passage and its companion Scripture, the parable of the pearl of great price.

- Where in Christianity is the "one very precious pearl"? How can we get to it?
- What is McLaren's plan for discovering that pearl?
- What does he mean by "conversion"? What is your response to the word "conversion" used in this context? Do you think Christianity needs a conversion?
- What is it about Christianity that has "too long been buried"?
- Do you feel hopeful about McLaren's vision?

Devotion

What You Love, You Protect

> *Timothy, guard what has been entrusted to you.*
> 1 Timothy 6:20 (NRSV)

> *Guard the good treasure entrusted to you, with the help of the Holy Spirit living in us.*
> 2 Timothy 1:14 (NRSV)

I live two miles from the Gulf of Mexico. Every summer, I serve as a volunteer sea turtle monitor. About once a week, early in the morning, I meet up with another volunteer or two and a marine biologist at a dock. We board a small boat and motor out to a stretch of pristine beaches on a six-mile string of uninhabited barrier islands. We look for the tracks of mother sea turtles who have dragged their bodies up the beach during the night, dug a nesting cavity, laid about a hundred eggs, and then returned to the sea.

We protect the eggs with a metal cage, and when the eggs hatch fifty to sixty days later, we dig up the nest and collect data on the number of eggs and hatchlings. Scientists use this data to help preserve sea turtles so the turtles can continue to fulfill their unique role in the ecosystems of our oceans, and so future generations of human beings can enjoy the miraculous creatures.

Our work is fun, and it's hard, too, with sunburn, mosquitos, fire ants, and challenging weather. But it's worth it, because it's a labor of love. All of us who volunteer do so because we have grown to love sea turtles. Because we care about them, we want to protect them—and to protect the environments upon which they depend.

What you love, you protect. And that's true of many things in life, including Christian faith.

I love the treasures of Christian faith. They have shaped me, guided me, and filled my life with meaning. It's because I love my faith that I want to protect it from the dangers it faces, because make no mistake, Christian faith is in danger.

The sea turtles in my area face many external threats: raccoons and hurricanes, shrimp nets and water pollution, and other forms of human interference from shoreline development to climate change.

In some parts of the world, Christian disciples also face many external threats—persecution, terrorism, imprisonment. But in most of the world, the greatest threats to Christianity are not external. They are internal. We Christians, you might say, are the greatest threat to Christian faith.

Christians can be blinded by wealth and greed, misguided by religious or political leaders, polluted by un-Christlike attitudes, kidnapped by ideology, or numbed by comfort and apathy. As a result, we can receive and pass on versions of the faith that are distorted with racism or twisted by greed or fear.

If we love our faith, we will seek to protect it from dangers like these. In the words of Paul to Timothy, we will guard the "good treasure that has been entrusted to us. If you think of faith as a baton that is handed from one generation to the next, you could say that those in each generation improve or degrade that baton while it is in their hands. Those in each generation pass on a better or worse version of the faith than the one they received. If previous generations went astray, we must engage in course correction. If we go astray, we must pray that future generations will not simply repeat our mistakes, but will have the courage to make corrections. Make no mistake: Christian faith will be what Christians make of it—ugly or beautiful, judgmental or gracious, complacent or energetic, selfish or generous. What will we pass on?

Living God, please teach me to abhor what is evil and love what is good. Help me to discern and leave behind imperfect and immature elements in the version of the faith I was given. And help me, together with my fellow disciples, to embody and pass on a vibrant version of the faith that will empower future generations to live wisely and well.

Brian McLaren

From a System of Beliefs to a Way of Life

Session 2

From a System of Beliefs
to a Way of Life

Summary

Part I: The Spiritual Migration: From a System of Beliefs to a Way of Life

When Brian McLaren set out to write *The Great Spiritual Migration*, he held the hope that Christianity might become more Christian. He maintains that the only thing that matters to many Christians is correct beliefs, and as a result they are missing the essential point of Christianity, which is that it should be defined as a way of life based on love, not just a system of beliefs. The Jesus we encounter in the Gospels wasn't all about right words or correct beliefs. He was about what we do, the fruit we bear, the houses we build on rock, the way we work for the will of God. Jesus was focused on the contents, not the container. And if we think that

Jesus was right, we have to let go of our obsession with opinions and beliefs. The essence of our faith is something different.

McLaren was serving as a pastor when he arrived at a desert retreat center to spend a few days with his colleagues. It was there that he had an earth-shaking realization: "My faith is a system of beliefs, and it's not working. The system is crumbling. I can't save it. I can't save it. It's over." McLaren found himself in a struggle between the faith that he loved and a system of beliefs he could no longer adhere to. Since he was a pastor, this was an especially difficult bind. There in the desert he looked for God's presence in the realization he'd just had. What he found was that maybe what really matters are not the beliefs Christians are told to proclaim, but the stories those beliefs came from. Maybe the narratives come before the system, and the stories are where the true treasures of the faith really lie.

The stories in the Bible contain "bottomless wells of meaning," McLaren observes, and he presents John's version of the story of Jesus' dramatic public protest in the Temple (John 2:13-22) as an example. According to most traditional interpretations of the story, Jesus was upset about the high cost of sacrifice. But McLaren looks more closely and finds that Jesus may have been overturning an entire system of belief, one that relied on the idea that God was angry and constantly needed to be appeased. Both the system of belief and the image of God were flawed. And even if the Temple falls, as Jesus says, it can rise again as something new. The falling Temple is the doorway to a new beginning. The same is true today for the system of beliefs called Christianity.

McLaren isn't rejecting Christian tradition when he questions the system of belief. Rather, he's suggesting that we focus more on the prophetic and poetic side of Christian tradition rather than the sides that claim doctrinal orthodoxy. Beliefs have served social and political functions that are often far removed from the stories and faith they come from. Christian faith needs to migrate from the system of beliefs it has been to a new place. It needs a radical conversion because beliefs are not the point. This is no quick fix, and McLaren is searching for deeper solutions.

Science has a lot to teach religion when it comes to being willing to test beliefs. When there is new evidence, Christianity must be willing to question even its most long-held beliefs. Christianity, McLaren says, must be willing to change its mind. He raises the issue of homosexuality as a case study. For a long time, homosexuality has been seen as a sin. But over time, the evidence has pointed to something different. McLaren drew from his own personal experience, considered cases he had heard of, and became willing to change his own view. To put it simply, Brian McLaren had both a Christian belief system and an ethic of love. If he kept to his belief about homosexuality being a sin, he would violate his ethic of love. His ethic of love became a foundational test, and it trumped his former belief. Christianity must be willing to make changes like this, and the ethic of love should always rule the day.

Calling for a shift from a rigid system of beliefs to a way of life based on love, McLaren looks to Jesus, who had plenty to say about love. In fact, love was at the center of nearly everything Jesus said and did. In the Sermon on the Mount (Matthew 5–7), Jesus says that God loves people unconditionally. Elsewhere, he talks about mercy, compassion, reconciliation, and other terms based on love. His actions (healing on the Sabbath, welcoming children, feeding the crowd) demonstrate that love takes precedence over everything. And his final message in the Gospel of John was, "Just as I have loved you, you also should love one another" (John 13:34, NRSV). Paul amplifies Jesus' message, emphasizing that faith matters more than correct beliefs. Both draw on what was already there in the biblical tradition, but they note that love is the foundational principle. Jesus and Paul call for a migration to love. If we accept this migration to love, then any view of God that doesn't lead to love must be false. And if we accept this migration to love, our whole understanding of church will be transformed.

Many people have been searching for a church that teaches a way of life rather than a system of beliefs. Churches that make this migration find the principle of love taught by Jesus to be the center of all practice. The first step is to love one's neighbor, and after loving family and friends comes love of outsider and enemy. Love for neighbor and love for self lead to love of the earth, which is also an essential part of a way of life of love.

This ethic of love becomes known through the rituals of a community: the words of welcome, common prayer, confession, creeds, Communion, sermons, offerings, songs, church design, and celebration of holidays. Imagine if all of these were configured and presented as expressions of love. Such a migration to love would change the way churches do their work, and all who gather would become apprentices of love and the life of Jesus.

SCRIPTURE REFLECTION

It was nearly time for the Jewish Passover, and Jesus went up to Jerusalem. He found in the temple those who were selling cattle, sheep, and doves, as well as those involved in exchanging currency sitting there. He made a whip from ropes and chased them all out of the temple, including the cattle and the sheep. He scattered the coins and overturned the tables of those who exchanged currency. He said to the dove sellers, "Get these things out of here! Don't make my Father's house a place of business." His disciples remembered that it is written, Passion for your house consumes me.

Then the Jewish leaders asked him, "By what authority are you doing these things? What miraculous sign will you show us?"

Jesus answered, "Destroy this temple and in three days I'll raise it up."

The Jewish leaders replied, "It took forty-six years to build this temple, and you will raise it up in three days?" But the temple Jesus was talking about was his body. After he was raised from the dead, his disciples remembered what he had said, and they believed the scripture and the word that Jesus had spoken.

John 2:13-22

Dear friends, let's love each other, because love is from God, and everyone who loves is born from God and knows God. The person who doesn't love does not know God, because God is love....

No one has ever seen God. If we love each other, God remains in us and his love is made perfect in us.

1 John 4:7-8, 12

I ask that he will strengthen you in your inner selves from the riches of his glory through the Spirit. I ask that Christ will live in your hearts through faith. As a result of having strong roots in love, I ask that you'll have the power to grasp love's width and length, height

and depth, together with all believers. I ask that you'll
know the love of Christ that is beyond knowledge so
that you will be filled entirely with the fullness of God.
                                                    Ephesians 3:16-19

Many traditional interpretations of the first passage, which is often called "the cleansing of the Temple," assume that Jesus is angry about how much it costs to buy animals for sacrifice. Jesus chases the sellers and money changers out of the Temple, the interpretation goes, because he is concerned about poor people who can't afford to buy animals for worship. Cattle, sheep, and doves were required for burnt offerings at the Temple, and for the Passover feast, many people would have traveled great distances without bringing animals with them. They would have needed to buy animals in Jerusalem, and they also would have needed to change currency in order to do so. The cost may have often been prohibitive, sparking Jesus' anger, as traditional interpretations suggest. In this case, though, the system was not necessarily corrupt; it was just carrying on as usual, although probably much busier than usual considering the holiday.

If Jesus really were angry about the high cost, he should have left the doves behind since they were the cheapest sacrifice option. But Jesus drives all the animals out, leaving none behind. Is there a deeper meaning to this story than just concern for the poor?

Jesus' confrontation appears in all four Gospels. Matthew, Mark, and Luke report that this happens near the end of Jesus' ministry in the days leading up to his crucifixion. But John places the incident at the beginning of Jesus' ministry, where it becomes a sign of what is to come: "Destroy this temple and in three days I'll raise it up" (2:19). With these words, Jesus makes a radical challenge to the authority of the Temple and its practices of worship.

But what if Jesus isn't angry about the cost of sacrifice, but rather about the entire *practice* of sacrifice? After all, the whole sacrificial system is based on the assumption that God is angry and must be appeased with animal sacrifice. This is not the God we see through the words and actions of Jesus. Perhaps Jesus is angry about what this system says about God. Perhaps he wants to overturn the sellers' tables right along with the entire system of beliefs in order to raise up something new in its place, the way of life of love.

McLaren writes, "Jesus is making a revolutionary proposal: the Temple could crumble. It could pass away, and its collapse wouldn't be the end of the world." Something better could rise in the place of the complicated system of beliefs based on sacrifice and appeasement of God. "A system of extravagant and generous grace, open to all people," McLaren continues. "A more human, loving, embodied way of relating to God, self, one another, and all creation."

In the same way, Christians shouldn't be afraid for the church to be challenged and even damaged. We can overturn tables and demand something better. It won't be the end of the world to look at the church and say that our systems of belief are not working anymore. We need a migration to a new way of life based on love. We need a better way of relating to God and each other. If the church crumbles, something new and better will rise up in its place. We have seen it happen before.

"Love" in the passage from 1 John is translated from the Greek *agape*, which can mean a human being's selfless love, the love of God through Christ, or even charitable love. It should be distinguished from *phileo*, which is brotherly love, and *eros*, which is romantic or sexual love. *Agape*, instead, is a universal, unconditional love that transcends and extends toward God. *Agape* is the primary word

Jesus uses for love throughout his ministry. In these words from 1 John, God is equated with *agape* love, and so the charge to love is a call to keep God close within us.

The author of 1 John echoes the love command given in Matthew:

> *"Teacher, what is the greatest commandment in the Law?"*
>
> *He replied*, "You must love [agape] the Lord your God with all your heart, with all your being, *and with all your mind. This is the first and greatest commandment. And the second is like it:* You must love [agape] your neighbor as you love yourself.
>
> *Matthew 22:36-39*

McLaren observes that with a tradition of Scripture like this, you would think love would always be at center stage in the Christian faith. Sadly, it is not. Instead, a focus on correct beliefs—loving or not—is what rules the day. McLaren offers the example of Pope Francis, whose emphasis on an ethic of love has faced resistance from centuries of tradition (and a centuries-old system of belief) that simply will not be altered or overturned. McLaren calls for a return to an emphasis on Scriptures like this one. He asks, "Are we ready to say that Christianity must no longer be defined by a list of unchanging beliefs, but rather by…a way of life centered in love, as embodied by Jesus?"

The passage from Paul's letter to the Ephesians maps out McLaren's vision for a new church that is based on love. Paul prays for believers to be strengthened in their inner selves with Christ living in their hearts. Strong roots in love will allow them to "grasp love's width and length, height and depth, together with all believers." Here we see the word *agape* used again and again, for the love of Christ and the love that will envelop and sustain the community of believers. If church members embrace the migration to the way of love, they will experience what Paul hopes for in this Scripture.

The way of life of love runs deep through the sacred writings of the New Testament and forms the basis of the emerging Christian faith. McLaren calls for a return to this emphasis, to practicing the way of love as Jesus taught. "Who develops, teaches, and refines a transformative curriculum of love?" McLaren asks. "If our churches don't do these things, who will?"

Questions for Reflection

1. The contrast between a way of life, or faith, and a system of belief is a key distinction for McLaren. When you look at your own religious experience, do you see a way of life or a system of belief? Is there a place for both?

2. Would you consider your tradition to be more of a system of belief or a way of life of love? What does Christianity mean to you in practical terms? What things define you as Christian?

3. How do you interpret Jesus' confrontation in the Temple? What do you think he was most angry about? Do you think his outburst was effective in changing people's minds?

4. If the Temple is a symbol for today's church, do you believe that it could crumble and rise again? How do you feel about the suggestion that the church is failing?

5. What do you think of the call to love in the passages from 1 John, Ephesians, and Matthew? Does today's church live into these words?

6. McLaren writes, "Only through loving neighbors do we prepare our hearts to love God. We might even say that the way to God runs through our neighbors—especially those who are vulnerable." What do you think of this connection between neighbor-love and the way to God? How do our churches already practice this, and where do they fall short?

7. The God who must be approached through a complex system of beliefs can seem distant and theoretical. What does the God of the way of life of love look like? How would approaching God through a new way of life change how the church does church?

8. Where did you learn what you know about love? How were you taught? How could your training in love have been improved?

9. McLaren's emphasis is not just on a new way of life, but a way of life of *love*. He suggests incorporating the message of love into all aspects of worship, from the welcome to prayer to communion, sermons, and songs. Would this change the worship service at your church? How might incorporating love at every step change how churches understand their relationship to God?

10. McLaren argues that the stories behind the system of beliefs, not the beliefs themselves, are where the true treasures of the faith can be found. What stories speak most powerfully to you? What teaches you about who Jesus is, who God is, and how to be a Christian, the stories you find in Scripture or a list of correct beliefs?

PERSONAL RESPONSE

It's high time for religious communities to learn a lesson from science. Could we adopt a willingness to question even long-held beliefs when new evidence arises? Could we allow our beliefs to be open to testing and improvement? Could we say that our religious communities are held together not by forever subscribing to the same beliefs, but by forever upholding the same passion to learn, even if new learning requires regularly admitting we were previously wrong?

-from The Great Spiritual Migration, Part I

> *Do not remember the former things,*
> *or consider the things of old.*
> *I am about to do a new thing;*
> *now it springs forth, do you not perceive it?*
> Isaiah 43:18-19 (NRSV)

In the above excerpt, Brian McLaren challenges Christians to apply the scientific method to their long-held system of beliefs. What would it be like to subject beliefs to the test when there is new evidence to indicate a need for change? The suggestion that some Christian beliefs could be wrong or might be due for question might feel uncomfortable for many believers, but McLaren insists that Christians must be capable of learning and changing their minds.

Reflect on your response to the above passage and its companion Scripture, Isaiah 43:18-19.

- What would it mean to you to question your Christian beliefs?

- Should Christianity subject its beliefs to evidence?
- What does McLaren suggest holds communities together if not beliefs?
- What do you think faith can learn from science?
- How do the words of God in Isaiah 43:18-19 relate to the above passage?
- How do you feel about talking about religion in terms of science? Or about "testing" your Christian beliefs?

DEVOTION

Supporting Characters

> *Remember your leaders, those who spoke the word of God to you; consider the outcome of their way of life, and imitate their faith.*
>
> Hebrews 13:7 (NRSV)

If your life were a movie, with you as the star, and if the plot of your movie were the story of you growing and maturing in love, who would the most important supporting characters be? Who modeled different facets of love for you?

In my life, as in many people's, my parents were my first models of love. They created a safe place in the world where I never had to doubt I was loved. What a gift that is!

My brother modeled the simple joy of companionship, along with the gift of forgiveness when I teased him or in other ways failed him.

A summer camp counselor was the first adult to see leadership potential in me. He imparted to me the sense that God had a special plan for my life.

Two pastors took me under their wing and mentored me as a young leader. They modeled lifelong growth and constant encouragement.

I think of my closest friends and the precious gifts of friendship they have given me.

I also think about heroes and saints from the past, people I never met in person, but whose life stories inspired me with examples of extraordinary love for God, neighbor, self, and the earth.

And of course, my wife would play a co-starring role because she has not only loved me, but also joined me in the adventure of loving our kids and now our grandkids.

In the Epistle to the Hebrews, we are encouraged to pay attention to the people who have modeled a faithful way of life for us to imitate. What an honor it would be for us to live in such a way that we could be supporting characters in the storyline of others' lives!

Maybe, the truth is that we aren't the stars of our own life story. Maybe we're all simply supporting characters for the real star: God, who is Love.

Living God, as Jesus walked this earth, he modeled a loving way of life for his disciples. They, in turn, modeled this way of life for the next generation, and the process has continued to this moment. Thank you for all those people whose lives have modeled love for me. Please, Holy Spirit, so fill me with your love that my life supports others through a positive example of love.

Brian McLaren

Session 3

Toward a
Loving God
of Liberation

Session 3

Toward a Loving God of Liberation

Summary

Part II: The Theological Migration: From a Violent God of Domination to a Nonviolent God of Liberation

In the second section of *The Great Spiritual Migration*, Brian McLaren demonstrates how throughout history, the violent image of God we see in the Bible has led to violent, oppressive behavior and anything but an ethic of love. This image of God, and this violent heritage, leads McLaren to wonder if Christianity is even salvageable. He concludes there is something at the heart of Christianity that is worth saving. But first Christians must face the violent past that was often reasoned and justified by the Bible. Christians who are migrating toward love are rejecting God as a violent Supreme Being and embracing a God who is

43

instead a powerful, renewing spirit at work for the common good.

McLaren traces the history of Christianity—and specifically the history of Christianity in America—to show how certain perceptions of God and understandings of Scripture led to great violence and depravity. He begins with events leading up to Columbus's arrival in the New World. Columbus and his crew were operating under Pope Nicholas V's 1452 proclamation, later called the "Doctrine of Discovery," which allowed Christians to take control of anything and anyone they "discovered" in their explorations. McLaren calls this doctrine the "genocide card." The Doctrine of Discovery opened the door to slavery, abuse, and domination of native peoples by establishing Christians and Christianity as supreme. Few spoke out against the egregious acts that were perpetrated on indigenous peoples.

As the New World was "discovered" and populated by European Christians, atrocities in the name of God continued to spread. Driven by an image of God who was violent, Christian, and approved of the terrible acts against native peoples, these early explorers considered themselves to be doing the work of religion. The suffering of African Americans and Native Americans at the hands of white Christians was justified by theological arguments positing white Christian supremacy as a biblical truth. Dangerous interpretations of Scripture continue to drive many Christians' worldviews, often unwittingly. The "dominion mandate" found in Genesis 1:28 is often the basis for cruel or destructive treatment of animals, the environment, and other people.

Our conceptions of God grow and develop over time and with maturity. Brian McLaren labels the stages in this development as leading up to "God 5.0." First he demonstrates how the God of supremacy—the one we call almighty, sovereign, king, supreme—is contrasted or rejected in Philippians 2, where Jesus empties himself and manifests the true nature of God. Throughout his ministry, Jesus empowered others, rejected violence and domination, overturned conventional ideas of supremacy and power, and was anything but a conquering king. To follow Jesus, then, is to change one's understanding of God. Jesus brought a radical new vision of God to the earth. And for the world to migrate toward a world of compassion and love, so must our vision of God.

On the way to this new vision of God—this God 5.0—we go through several stages:

1. God 1.0 attended to your every need, much like your parents when you were an infant. Since adults came to your aid whenever you called, you developed a primal trust in God 1.0.
2. As you grew into a toddler and learned to make others laugh, share toys, and bring happiness to others, you grew toward God 2.0. It was a move from selfishness to generosity. This God wanted you to be polite and generous and play well with others.
3. Later at school, you encountered lots and lots of rules. This was the world of God 3.0, the God who would reward the rule-keepers and punish the rule-breakers.
4. Next came God 4.0, along with a first romance and first love. You learned how to navigate the world with a significant other always in mind. God 4.0 was a God of affection and family.

But God 4.0, beautiful as it is, isn't enough. God 4.0 is the God of the *exclusive we*, the one who takes care of *us* but not *them*. We have graduated to *we, us, ourselves* and moved past *me, myself,* and *mine*, but it still isn't enough. We must look beyond ourselves, and understand that God is also looking beyond our small enclosure.

5. We need God 5.0, who is the God of the "inclusive we." We need this God to keep us from war, to keep us together, to teach us to care for the earth. We need God 5.0 because we are all part of one family tree and we need an understanding of God that reflects that reality.

Making our way to God 5.0 doesn't mean abandoning what's in the Bible. The God of Jesus *is* God 5.0. Jesus is all about the inclusive we. Embracing God 5.0 means embracing Jesus and everything he wanted for us and emptied himself out for. And embracing God 5.0 doesn't mean abandoning previous visions of God or the lessons we learned from them. Rather, "our new concepts of God can acknowledge and incorporate the tragic misunderstandings and mistakes of our past and seek to become stronger through them." It's an integral change, not a wholesale rejection. Seeking the God that Jesus knew and embodied is a better way of being Christian. This is the theological migration.

But Scripture often presents God as violent, while in other places it shows God as merciful and gentle and kind. What are we to do with this contrast? Like many Christians, Brian McLaren grew up with the idea of biblical inerrancy. If the Bible said it happened, then it happened. The only other option was a liberal read of the Bible, which back then he surely didn't want! But over time he learned that there are a number of ways to approach the biblical text. He imagines a spectrum stretching out between literal— the Bible contains objective facts and metaphysical truths—and literary—the Bible has changing contexts, metaphorical truths, and a collection of stories that have various meanings. A literal view sees the Bible as a source of information. A literary view sees the Bible and its stories as sources of meaning. Reading in the literary way allows the Bible to be constantly giving birth to new meaning and new insights.

McLaren writes, "I was given permission to migrate from the limited universe of the conventional, exclusive, and often violent Supreme Being to the ever-expanding universe of a more awesome and wonderful God, all while keeping my Bible firmly in hand." And for those who worry if changing the way we read the Bible means losing hold of Jesus, that's not the case. Reading God through Jesus, for example, reveals a generous God who is always with us. If we migrate to this way of reading Scripture, "the Bible can become an expansive library of texts in travail that give birth to a new vision of God, a new way of life and mission, and a new chapter in the story of Christian faith."

Scripture Reflection

God blessed them and said to them, "Be fertile and multiply; fill the earth and master it. Take charge of the fish of the sea, the birds in the sky, and everything crawling on the ground."

Genesis 1:28

Don't do anything for selfish purposes, but with humility think of others as better than yourselves. Instead of each person watching out for their own good, watch out for what is better for others. Adopt the attitude that was in Christ Jesus:

> *Though he was in the form of God,*
> *he did not consider being equal with God*
> *something to exploit.*

But he emptied himself
by taking the form of a slave
and by becoming like human beings.
When he found himself in the form of a human,
he humbled himself by becoming obedient
to the point of death,
even death on a cross.
Therefore, God highly honored him
and gave him a name above all names,
so that at the name of Jesus everyone
in heaven, on earth, and under the earth
might bow
and every tongue confess that
      Jesus Christ is Lord, to the glory of
      God the Father.

                    Philippians 2:3-11

So then, if anyone is in Christ, that person is part
of the new creation. The old things have gone away,
and look, new things have arrived!

                    2 Corinthians 5:17

[God] has told you, human one, what is good and
what the LORD *requires from you:*
    to do justice, embrace faithful love, and
    walk humbly with your God.

                    Micah 6:8

Genesis 1:28 is often referred to as the "dominion mandate." Used as a justification for taking control of everything from animals to land and water to native people in yet undiscovered places, this verse has for centuries told human beings—and specifically

Christians—that they have the right to dominate. "Take charge" is more commonly translated as "have dominion over" (NRSV, KJV, ESV) or "rule over" (NIV). In the age of exploration, the Bible was used to justify the "Doctrine of Discovery," a pronouncement by Popes in the 15th century that the entire world was ruled by the Pope and the Catholic Church, who reigned as God's representative on earth. As such, any land that was not already under Christian rule could be possessed and controlled on behalf of God. Sadly, this was the beginning of great suffering for those native people who were already living in the New World when explorers arrived. There was also great suffering for those who were captured and enslaved in Africa under the same kind of justification.

Brian McLaren calls for a theological migration that moves away from this kind of violent and dominating interpretation of Scripture. He writes, "To be converted from all forms of supremacy and domination, we must dare to embark on a great theological migration, challenging many of our deepest assumptions about God."

The Hebrew word for "take charge," "have dominion over," or "rule" is *radah*, and it refers to governing action, like that of a king. The same word appears in Psalm 72: "Let the king rule from sea to sea,/ from the river to the ends of the earth" (verse 8). But look more closely at this psalm. The description of dominion is more detailed and the implications of rule are made clear.

> *Let all the kings bow down before him;*
> *let all the nations serve him.*

> *Let it be so, because he delivers the needy who cry out,*
> *the poor, and those who have no helper.*
> *He has compassion on the weak and the needy;*
> *he saves the lives of those who are in need.*

He redeems their lives from oppression and violence;
their blood is precious in his eyes.

Psalm 72:11-14

The king who is celebrated in these verses does something quite different with his dominion. He delivers the needy, he helps the poor, he has compassion, and he saves lives. Most importantly, he redeems lives from oppression and violence. This is a king who deserves honor not because of his power and might, but his gentleness and kindness. If this king is meant to represent God, this is a very different vision of God than the one invoked by explorers and early Americans.

If this is the ideal kind of dominion, what kind of *radah* is not acceptable? Ezekiel offers a scathing description: "You don't strengthen the weak, heal the sick, bind up the injured, bring back the strays, or seek out the lost; but instead you use force to rule them with injustice" (34:4). This is exactly the kind of dominion we often see in history, and it's away from this superior and dominating stance that we must migrate. The dominion that God desires is reflected in Psalm 72, one that seeks protection for the weak rather than dominating them, that helps the poor rather than exploiting them, and that saves lives rather than causing suffering and death to others. Psalm 72 reflects "God 5.0," the God of the inclusive we, who cares for everyone and defines dominion as responsibility and care rather than subjugation and violence.

Unfortunately, the dominion mandate in Genesis 1:28 has been interpreted as a call to dominate. But what if the charge to "master" the earth and "take charge" of all the creatures had been taken as a call to responsibility? What if "take charge" could mean take care rather than lord over? What if we envisioned a God who embraced everyone and called for us to do the same? This is the God of the way of life of love.

The Christ Hymn, as the passage from Philippians is often called, presents the voluntary humiliation of Jesus followed by his exaltation. What is described in the first part is called *kenosis*, or the emptying out of one's will to become entirely receptive of God's will. It is the ultimate in humility. Christians are called to adopt this attitude, in which Jesus, knowing he was in the form of God, did not consider that power and status something to exploit. Jesus humbled himself to the point of becoming like human beings, and being obedient even until he suffered death on the cross. This attitude of humility, this "watching out for what is better for others," is the opposite of the dominating supremacy enacted in the name of God by so many Christians across history. The Christ Hymn rejects that kind of dominion and calls for a migration to something new. The God reflected by Jesus in these lines is the God of the inclusive we.

The new creation announced in 2 Corinthians is what awaits us as we migrate to a new way of life based on love. In our life in Jesus, we should never again compare God to kings or rulers who hold violent dominion, exploit people, or marginalize the weak or outcast among us. The great spiritual migration, including these crucial theological shifts, brings us to an entirely new world where dominating supremacy is a thing of the past. The new creation undoes harmful interpretations of the "dominion mandate" found in the Genesis creation story and calls for humility, compassion, and love.

And yet calls for humility, compassion, and love are not new to Jesus or the New Testament. What the great spiritual migration calls for is not a rejection of the past, but a building and improving and strengthening of the best of the traditions that already shape us. In Micah 6:8, it is God's desire that we do justice, embrace faithful love, and walk humbly with God. This is also part of the new creation. This is also the way of life of love. Jesus knew his Hebrew Scriptures, and he never meant for us to abandon them. What McLaren calls for is more careful reading, new interpretations, and a rejection of images of God that don't feed and nourish the new way of life of love.

QUESTIONS FOR REFLECTION

1. How do you reconcile the contrasting images found in the Bible, the God who is sometimes violent and taking sides versus the God who is loving, protective, and kind?
2. What is your take on McLaren's progression from God 1.0 to God 5.0? Where do you land on that spectrum? Do you think Christians should be aiming for God 5.0, the God of the inclusive we?
3. Were you surprised to learn how much violence and domination in history—including early American history—was perpetrated by Christians using the Bible as justification? What do you think of the relationship between the Bible and these shameful moments in our past?
4. Have you ever heard of the Doctrine of Discovery? What about the "dominion mandate"? How does knowing about these concepts change your reading of the creation story in Genesis?
5. What do you think it means in Genesis 1:28 for human beings to "take charge" of the earth and all its creatures?

6. We are given different views of God in both the Old Testament and the New Testament. Why do you think some passages portray God as purely kind and others as sometimes cruel? How does McLaren suggest we reconcile those competing visions?
7. How does the humility of Christ, described in the Christ Hymn in Philippians, reflect the image of God 5.0?
8. How does the Christ Hymn provide a model for how we might envision God and move forward in a new way of life?
9. What is your image of God? Father? mother? friend? How has reading this chapter challenged some of your understandings of God?
10. Do you think Christianity can migrate to become the renewed faith McLaren envisions? Try defending the position opposite to the one you would normally support, and see how things look from that perspective.

PERSONAL RESPONSE

When Moses is given the Ten Commandments, he doesn't say that Abraham's religion was wrong because he didn't have them. And when Solomon builds an elaborate temple of stone, he doesn't say Moses's religion was wrong because he had only a tent of cloth. And when the prophets Amos, Isaiah, and Micah come along, they don't advocate rejecting their religion and culture, even though they are highly critical of its spiritual hypocrisy and social injustice. They want their religion to expand, to evolve, to learn and grow. The same is true with Jesus.

-from *The Great Spiritual Migration,* Part II

Do not think that I have come to abolish the law or
the prophets; I have come not to abolish but to fulfill.

Matthew 5:17 (NRSV)

The above excerpt from *The Great Spiritual Migration* describes the progression of change and improvement within religion. The process is sometimes painful, often fraught with controversy, and always ongoing. Brian McLaren uses this example to describe how individuals and churches might migrate to "God 5.0" and embrace what he calls a "larger, grander, inclusive God."

Reflect on your response to the above passage and its companion Scripture, Matthew 5:17.

- How do you think of the movement from one tradition to another in the Bible?
- What is your image of God?
- Do you think that changing how people think of God will change how they behave?
- How do Jesus' words relate to the excerpt from McLaren?
- What would it mean to admit that parts of Christianity have been wrong?
- In what ways is it necessary for Christianity "to expand, to evolve, to learn and grow"?
- What is the new vision of God brought by Jesus?

DEVOTION

Nonviolent God

Long ago God spoke to our ancestors in many and
various ways by the prophets, but in these last days
he has spoken to us by a Son, whom he appointed

heir of all things, through whom he also created the worlds. He is the reflection of God's glory and the exact imprint of God's very being…

Hebrews 1:1-3 (NRSV)

[Christ] is the image of the invisible God, the first-born of all creation;… For in him all the fullness of God was pleased to dwell, and through him God was pleased to reconcile to himself all things, whether on earth or in heaven, by making peace through the blood of his cross.

Colossians 1:15, 19-20 (NRSV)

The great theologians of history have told us that no single image for God is enough to contain God. We need a variety of images to supplement and even correct each other. We see this pattern play out in Scripture.

For example, many biblical writers refer to God as King. This accurately reflects God's power and majesty. But we have to be careful because many kings in history have been power-hungry and tawdry in character, committing acts of hate, injustice, torture, and killing.

That's why Jesus often used a different image for God: that of a caring father whose heart is generous and eager to forgive. But we must acknowledge that some fathers are stern, even cruel.

That's why Jesus also gave us the image of a mother hen, gathering her chicks, willing to suffer and even die for their protection. In this, he was imitating some of the prophets of past generations who imaged God as a mother.

But even the images of king, father, and mother can't fully reflect God. That's why Jesus used so many other images, too: a friend, a vineyard keeper, light, living water, even wine.

It's clear that for Jesus, any violent image for God needed to be corrected and left behind. Any image of God that portrayed God as prejudiced for some people and against others needed to be corrected and left behind. That's why the ultimate image he gave us to understand God was himself. "Whoever has seen me has seen the Father," he said.

How many people did Jesus turn away? How many did he shame? Who did he try to dehumanize, torture, exploit, or kill?

When I was growing up, I was taught that the ultimate Word or expression or revelation of God was a book, the Bible. As a result, I thought that every violent image of God that was in the Bible must be true.

Later I learned that the ultimate Word or expression or revelation of God is not a book but a person, Jesus. That helped me see that Jesus' nonviolent life most radiantly reveals the character of God, and it corrects any and all violent images of God, wherever they are found.

Past prophets spoke of God in various ways, but the New Testament says (Hebrews 1:3) that in Jesus, God is revealed most accurately and fully: "[Jesus] is the radiance of God's glory and the exact representation of his being" (NIV).

We often say that we are created in God's image. The truth is, whatever our image or understanding of God, we will tend to become like it. If our understanding of God is violent and cruel, we will indeed be conformed to that image. If our understanding of God is compassionate and gracious, we will be conformed to that image.

The reverse can also be true. If we are harsh and heartless people, we will tend to see God as harsh and heartless, making God in our image.

Can you see why it is so important for us to understand God as imaged in Jesus, a nonviolent man who never shamed, harmed, tortured, or killed anyone?

God, help me to see your glory reflected in the face of Jesus, and help me be transformed into that image, from glory to glory. And God, help me reflect your glory to others, so they will see the fruit of my life and understand how good you are—kind, generous, gracious, true, just, merciful, and full of the purest light of love, with no darkness at all.

Brian McLaren

Session 4

For the
Common Good

Session 4

For the Common Good

SUMMARY

Part III: The Missional Migration: From Organized Religion to Organizing Religion

With a change in the way we see God and Scripture comes the call for a new way of life. Christianity is no longer a simple system of beliefs. To demonstrate how this can happen, Brian McLaren imagines churches and organizations forming social movements. He uses social movement theory to explain both how churches and organizations might make the migration to a new way of life, and to shed light on how Jesus and his followers accomplished what they did.

First, movement leaders find the "opportunity structure." This means they identify the context and incentives that make the movement necessary and possible. Current dissension among religious groups is part of that, along with globalism and the Internet. Next come "rhetorical framing and conceptual architecture." More clearly stated, that's how we tell our stories and how we explain what and why the movement is liberating. "Mobilizing structures" provide clear lines of communication and opportunities for relationship building within the movement. Most of all, a movement must be "an experimental field where people can actually observe and experience the new way of life it advocates." The movement has to reflect something real. And finally, the movement must make a difference not only in the world, but in the lives of the people involved, building their "participant biographies." Brian McLaren asks,

> What kind of spiritual movement could challenge willing sectors of Christian faith to migrate from their systems of belief to a shared way of life centered in love? I wondered. What kind of theological movement could help us migrate from conventional violent understandings of God to the nonviolent vision of God embodied in Jesus? And how could these changes in spirituality and theology be expressed as a transformative movement in the culture at large?

In a sense, Jesus started a social movement with his work in the Gospels. Jesus saw the opportunity for change and seized it. He used a powerful image to communicate his message (the Kingdom of God), practiced a unique form of storytelling (parables), and used catchy slogans ("Love your neighbor," "Take up your cross"). He taught and demonstrated publicly (the Sermon on the Mount, the feeding of the five thousand), and he trained the disciples.

His mobilizing structures included the disciples in various configurations. The movement culture was characterized by feasts, parties, joyful processions, and outdoor festivals. Women were given much responsibility. Those who were outcast were included. And the New Testament contains the participant biographies of many of those who were caught up in the movement. Social movement, indeed!

This pattern of organizing recurs throughout Christian history, in people like St. Francis; the Wesleys; Martin Luther King, Jr.; and Desmond Tutu. Catholics and Protestants went through movements of formation, leading sometimes to schism and the birth of new denominations. Christianity is always in the process of moving itself, including the recent rise of the so-called "religious right," which has been characterized by many of the social movement qualities discussed here. But Christianity can't save itself by being further splintered. Rather, various movements across all Christianity must come together and solve what is not really a Christian problem, but a human one.

The primary concern for many Christians is the fate of our churches. And tied to the fate of our churches is the precarious fate of our earth. We have an endless amount of greed, but we don't have an endless amount of fossil fuels to satisfy all those desires. The earth is suffering under our weight, and Christianity as a system of beliefs has been largely oblivious to the problem. The salvation lies in the third migration: "from *a religion organized for self-preservation and privilege to a religion organizing for the common good of all.*"

Toward this migration, McLaren presents the following charges:

- Christian communities that are engaging this migration should speak up, and other Christians should start new communities where there are none.
- Christian leaders and parents should start with children and young people so that they are familiar with the ideas of the movement from the beginning.
- Christian communities should seek different leaders and train them differently.

The migration from a system of beliefs to a way of life of love, from organized religion to organizing religion, will not just wash over us. It is waiting for us to get organized, build the ship, and direct ourselves and our movement where we need to go. Christianity is salvageable, but it will take our careful thought and effort to save it.

But how can we move the great spiritual migration to a new way of life centered in love from a dream to a reality? Change begins inside people. And that change within people must lead to a broader change among people, followed by a change in institutions, and a change in our very culture. Churches have a big role to play in shaping these changes, but many remain complacent about the work they could be doing. One way in which individuals and institutions can effect change is through economic activism—boycotts, protests, social entrepreneurship, ethical divestment—strategies that work for change by targeting power structures.

McLaren borrows the term "social poets" from Pope Francis to describe those who begin the work of change in their communities. This move toward organizing religion forces Christians to ask important questions about the environment, the poor and the vulnerable, ongoing conflicts, and how to promote the social good as they shape a new reality. For such a movement to succeed, multifaith collaboration is essential. Every religion has its own gifts to bring to this change of heart for the common good. The great spiritual migration we need calls for these groups and individuals to become social poets of change, "sincere and creative people who will rise on the wings of faith to catch the wind of the Spirit."

But spiritual migration is difficult. The way of migration is also the way of the cross, and hearts will be broken along the way. But for things to change, we must be willing to suffer the birth pains of a new reality. McLaren returns to the story of Jesus in the Temple in the Gospel of John. His actions in the story are disruptive, much like the rest of Jesus' ministry. The great spiritual migration also requires disruption and tearing down of old and destructive systems of belief, much like Jesus predicted the crumbling of the Temple and the rise of something new in its place. McLaren suggests that the change begins with people. The great spiritual migration begins in the body of each individual person who longs for liberation and change.

SCRIPTURE REFLECTION

Then Jesus said to his disciples, "All who want to come after me must say no to themselves, take up their cross, and follow me. All who want to save their lives will lose them. But all who lose their lives because of me will find them."

Matthew 16:24-25

You yourselves are being built like living stones into a spiritual temple. You are being made into a holy priesthood to offer up spiritual sacrifices that are acceptable to God through Jesus Christ.

1 Peter 2:5

*Christ is just like the human body—a body is a unit
and has many parts; and all the parts of the body
are one body, even though there are many. We were
all baptized by one Spirit into one body, whether Jew
or Greek, or slave or free, and we all were given one
Spirit to drink. Certainly the body isn't one part but
many.*

1 Corinthians 12:12-14

In the passage from the Gospel of Matthew, Jesus offers strong words to the disciples who are following him. We can only imagine what the disciples must have been thinking. Take up a cross? Lose our lives? Indeed, the call may well have been to martyrdom, which was something that happened in Matthew's church and has happened to Christians since. But there is also a promise hidden in these words: "All who lose their lives because of me will find them" (16:25). There is new life to be found at the end of the old life. Change is coming.

The call to discipleship is a matter of community. The point is not that the disciples must be willing to die in order to follow Jesus, but that they are willing to give up everything they value to enter into a new life. The cost of discipleship is great. Just as the members of the greatest social movements in our history can attest, in many ways they had to give up their lives in order to find them. Giving up one's life means turning oneself over to the community and saying that others are more important. The members of any movement must make enormous sacrifices in order to stand up for their cause.

But what about those "who want to save their lives"? Isn't that the human instinct? Why would they then *lose* their lives? Here Jesus gives a warning to those who are living selfishly and think they have no need to change anything. These are the people who are so mired in their systems of belief that they refuse to consider the possibility of anything else. These are the Christians who say no to the way of life of love. They try to save their lives as they are, and ultimately they will lose them as their system of belief crumbles around them.

This reflection in Matthew on the meaning of discipleship—indeed, the very meaning of being *Christian*—calls believers to put their lives on the line for Jesus. In the Gospel of Luke, Jesus is even more specific about what it will take to follow him: "Whoever comes to me and doesn't hate father and mother, spouse and children, and brothers and sisters—yes, even one's own life—cannot be my disciple" (14:26). This is not martyrdom, but a radical giving up of possessions and personal goals and relationships for the sake of the movement.

What if it's the church's life that must be lost in order to be found? "Could our desire to save our precious religious institutions and traditions actually hasten their demise?" McLaren asks. "Could it be that the spirit of God is calling the church to stop trying to save itself, and instead to join God in saving the world? Could pouring out itself for the good of the world be the only way for the church to save its own soul?" It is not organized religion that needs to be saved. It is organizing religion that must grow and flourish.

The "living stones" of 1 Peter may hold the answer. Now that the old sacrificial system is gone, the only thing we need is a living sacrifice, giving up our bodies—and yes, our lives—as a gift to God. All the participants in the movement for a way of life of love come together to form a new spiritual temple out of their lives as living stones. The new church is made up of all of these individual bodies, and the spiritual sacrifices are what must be given up to be a disciple. The old way of life gives way to something new, a way of life based on love. McLaren writes, "The way of life centered in the Temple must be disrupted because God wanted to dwell not in buildings of bricks or stones cemented together by mortar, but rather in human beings...cemented together by mutual love, honor and respect." The buildings of bricks or stone cemented together by mortar are still standing today, and moving around inside are systems of belief rather than conduits of love. Bringing down the Temple is not a statement against the Jewish faith, but rather a once-and-for-all call for religion to be a way of life of love rather than a rigid collection of beliefs and practices.

The verses from First Corinthians paint an even more vivid portrait of the church as constructed out of living beings. Christ is just like the human body, made up of many parts. And each of us in the community of believers is a part of the body of Christ. Our bodies make up the movement and the community and the church, which is the very enactment of Christ on this earth. The great spiritual migration is made up of all of us, "with all of our doubts and imperfections, all of our failures, fears, and flaws," as McLaren describes. "You. Me. Everyone. No exceptions."

The movement to a new way of life based on love—away from a rigid system of beliefs, away from a violent, dominating God—is a "disruptive revolution" that is already beginning. Every part, every voice is essential. It is open to anyone, any race, any religion, any level of wealth or poverty or power. The great spiritual migration has room for everyone. This is the way of life, the body of Christ moving ever surer toward its ultimate place of life and peace, the way of life announced and lived by Jesus.

QUESTIONS FOR REFLECTION

1. McLaren sees Christianity as constantly moving and changing. What changes—positive and negative—have you seen in Christianity across your own lifetime? What changes would you like to see?
2. Have you ever been involved in a social movement? What elements of social movement theory characterize your experience with church?
3. How would you feel about being a part of the great spiritual migration? Do you believe that the church is ready for this kind of change?
4. Jesus makes the radical claim that to follow him, you must lose your life. What do you think that means? Are you prepared to lose your life to follow Jesus?
5. McLaren describes "social poets" as creative people who are working in the world to effect change such as members of social movements, advocates for the weak and vulnerable, or anyone creating meaning and change for the common good. In what ways are you a social poet?
6. What is the difference between organized religion and organizing religion? How will the migration from one to the other change the church?
7. McLaren describes his vision and spirituality as "disruptive." How do you understand that term in this context? Is disruption always negative?
8. The goal of the great spiritual migration is for Christianity to be "organizing for the common good." In what ways does the church already organize for the common good, and how could it do better?

9. McLaren writes that there is "so much right with the world." Is the same true for Christianity? What do you think the church gets right?

10. What is the ultimate outcome that McLaren is hoping for? To ask what he calls "a dangerous question," what do the churches of the future look like?

PERSONAL RESPONSE

If you want to see the future of Christianity as a great spiritual migration, don't look at a church building. Go look in the mirror and look at your neighbor. God's message of love is sent into the world in human envelopes. If you want to see a great spiritual migration begin, then let it start right in your body. Let your life be a foothold of liberation.

-from *The Great Spiritual Migration*, Part III

Now there was a woman who had been suffering from hemorrhages for twelve years; and though she had spent all she had on physicians, no one could cure her. She came up behind him and touched the fringe of his clothes, and immediately her hemorrhage stopped. Then Jesus asked, "Who touched me?" When all denied it, Peter said, "Master, the crowds surround you and press in on you." But Jesus said, "Someone touched me; for I noticed that power had gone out from me." When the woman saw that she could not remain hidden, she came trembling; and falling down before him, she declared in the presence of all the people why she had touched him, and how she had been immediately healed. He said to her, "Daughter, your faith has made you well; go in peace."

Luke 8:43-48 (NRSV)

The above excerpt from *The Great Spiritual Migration* empha-sizes that the migration begins with each individual Christian. The answer is not in a church building or other organization; the answer is in the mirror. Our loving God speaks through human bodies, and we make the choice to participate.

The above excerpt from *The Great Spiritual Migration* emphasizes that the migration begins with each individual Christian. The answer is not in a church building or other organization; the answer is in the mirror. Our loving God speaks through human bodies, and we make the choice to participate.

Reflect on your response to the above passage and its companion Scripture, the story of the hemorrhaging woman boldly reaching for healing from Jesus.

- Why is it important for the great spiritual migration to begin with individuals?
- What does it mean that "God's message of love is sent in human envelopes"?
- How does Luke's story of the hemorrhaging woman relate to the excerpt from McLaren?
- Why must human beings lead the change McLaren calls for?
- The hemorrhaging woman reaches out to touch Jesus in order to get the healing her body needs. How does her action symbolize the kind of movement required for the great spiritual migration?

Devotion

Organizing Religion

> *Your kingdom come.*
> *Your will be done,*
> *on earth as it is in heaven.*
> > *Matthew 6:10 (NRSV)*

When I was a boy, I wasn't very good at sports. But I remember two great sports experiences in secondary school. It turned out that even though I didn't run very fast, I was pretty good at pitching a softball. So I became a pitcher and even got a nickname from my teammates: B-Mac. Later, I joined a soccer team, and although I wasn't by any means a star, and although I think our team lost more games than we won, I loved the experience of doing my part to help us play our best.

My forte as a teenager was music. I loved playing in a symphonic band (clarinet), a jazz band (saxophone) and a few rock-and-roll bands (sax and later guitar).

In adulthood, I've learned the joy of working for a variety of causes that I care about. I have helped oppose the death penalty, mass incarceration, and solitary confinement. I have marched and advocated for the well-being of vulnerable people, including people who are diversely abled, people who are not heterosexual, migrant farm workers, undocumented immigrants, and people who are of minority races and religions. I have been arrested in an act of civil disobedience on behalf of the poor, and I have worked hard in a number of environmental causes.

All these experiences involved belonging, teamwork, good organization, and a common purpose.

In sports, the purpose was winning (or at least not losing too badly!). In music, the purpose was making beautiful music and bringing joy to our audiences (and often, truth be told, impressing girls). In my activism, the purpose has been contributing to the common good.

One of our great opportunities in church life these days is to rediscover our purpose as God's team, God's band, God's movement of activists.

Sadly, many people have lost sight of the purpose for church life, or they are working hard for the wrong purposes. They may act as if God wakes up every seven days or so with a terrible headache that only a liturgy of preludes, confessions, and creeds can heal, or that God slips into depression unless enough of us try to lift God's flagging self-esteem with lots of adulation. No wonder so many people are dropping out of church!

But imagine what could happen if we truly rediscovered the purpose (or mission) of the church. How would you put that into words?

I used to think our purpose was to intercept souls bound for hell so we could get them to say a simple prayer that would change their destination.

For a while, I acted as if the purpose of the church was to fill as many seats as possible each Sunday.

At times, I have felt, somewhat cynically, that the purpose of the church was to keep clergy employed, or to mobilize people for a political party or an economic ideology.

Now, I am convinced that the purpose of the church is to join God in the healing of the world.

Of course that healing begins with us. We need to experience the inner healing that the world needs...healing from greed, fear, apathy, and shame; healing from guilt, lust, and bitterness; healing from racism, nationalism, and materialism. That inner healing naturally enlists us for the team, band, and movement of God to extend that healing to everyone who is ready for it, so that the systems and structures of our world reflect God's will.

I dream of the day when our churches aren't simply organized to complete a liturgical checklist or keep a clergy guild employed. I dream of the day when our churches organize people to join

God in the healing of the world, beginning (but not ending!) with ourselves.

There are few things in life better than belonging, teamwork, good organization, and a common purpose, especially when the purpose is God's will being done on earth as it is in heaven!

Living God, your Son Jesus started a movement, and your Spirit has been empowering and guiding that movement ever since. But often, we part ways with the direction of your movement, and we keep our religion going like a well-oiled machine, organized for the wrong purposes. I present myself like a player to a coach, like a musician to a conductor, and like an activist to you, our leader. Help me get in sync with the movement of your Spirit, a movement for justice, joy, and peace, so I can join you in the healing of this beloved world.

Brian McLaren

Conclusion

Conclusion

Brian McLaren's call for the great spiritual migration is a daunting one. Who among us wants to take the lead to change a tradition grounded in centuries of tradition? Who wants to speak up in the quiet sanctuary of church and say that things have to change? It seems disruptive and impossible. But disruption is exactly what McLaren is calling for.

Throughout the book, McLaren recalls the voice of God that spoke within him as he began to think about the great spiritual migration: "*Get going! Go farther! Go forward!*" Great migrations have happened across Christian history. Now is the time. He writes, "The call to get moving comes not after the way is clear, but while it still seems impassable."

The concepts are not complicated ones. We must look at how our religious tradition has become centered on a rigid system of beliefs, and question that. Shouldn't Christianity be about following Jesus and emulating his way of life of love? Shouldn't we *live* Christianity rather than just *believe* in it? We must also make a close examination of our conception of God and question why we see God as vengeful and violent when there is so much evidence to the contrary. We must let our image of a loving, generous God be the guiding force in how we treat the world and each other. Finally, we must believe that we can effect change. We must live the way of life and embrace a vision of a loving God. The movement must begin, and we must get it started.

As we think through these questions, McLaren is sure, we can find a better way to be Christian and a better way to be human. It may be a difficult journey, as most migrations are. There will be wind and weather, and it will be hard to stay together in formation and reach the destination. But "through suffering and loss, through disruption and grief, through the way of the cross," McLaren writes, we "finally see that everything is holy. And in this way, to be alive and free."

Made in the USA
Las Vegas, NV
03 December 2021

35953391R00046